IMAGES OF WALES

AROUND
OLD COLWYN

IMAGES OF WALES

# AROUND
# OLD COLWYN

PATRICK SLATTERY

TEMPUS

*I would like to dedicate this book to Old Colwyn Junior School where I was educated from 1951-1960. It was there I learnt to appreciate and take an interest in the area where I was born.*

*All the author's royalties will be donated to the Old Colwyn Junior School.*

First published 2007

Tempus Publishing
Cirencester Road, Chalford,
Stroud, Gloucestershire, GL6 8PE
www.tempus-publishing.com

Tempus Publishing is an imprint of NPI Media Group

British Library Cataloguing in Publication Data.
A catalogue record for this book is available from the British Library.

ISBN 978 0 7524 3969 3

Typesetting and origination by NPI Media Group
Printed in Great Britain

# Contents

# Acknowledgements

For a number of years I have dreamt of publishing a book of old pictures of Colwyn Bay area. This book would not have been published without the generosity of Peter Clough who has most kindly loaned me his late father's collection of photograph albums of the Colwyn Bay area. I am greatly indebted to him for his help and permission to use many photos from this interesting and extensive personal collection which has made this book become a reality.

I am most grateful to Tempus Publishing Ltd, for their patience and guidance to me with my preparations and am delighted it will be part of the Images of Wales series of books published by such a reputable company.

# Introduction

From an early age I have taken an interest in the history and development of the village of Old Colwyn on the North Wales coast where I was born and spent thirty-seven very happy years. As a teenager I read avidly all the local papers and began to collect newspaper cuttings of anything relating to Old Colwyn. As the collection grew I began to stick cuttings into scrap books and soon had a large collection.

Old Colwyn was a large village and had seen little change during the 1950s to the 1970s, although I do remember watching with interest the building scheme below the Queens Hotel. Wynn Drive and Wynn Crescent were unique as they were the first bungalows to be built in Old Colwyn. I can remember the building contractor G.C. Jones of Llysfaen preparing the site and digging a large lime pit which was soon filled with lime in preparation for making mortar. A great transformation in the early 1960s was the phasing out of gas lights on the streets and replacing them with electric lights and the building of the new sea wall as part of the coastal protection scheme from Old Colwyn to

Tan Lan. What is remarkable is that large numbers of workmen were employed to use picks and shovels to dig lime pits, trenches to bury electric cables and foundations for sea walls. Today a mechanical digger would be used. In retrospect I regret I never had a camera in those days to take some pictures of these projects and the way those men laboured and toiled. Health and safety regulations had not been dreamt of; waterproof clothing was not supplied and the only protection from wet weather was an old raincoat with a hessian sack over the shoulders tied at the front. This was the gear the men who worked in Penmaenrhos Quarry wore on wet days as they manhandled rocks in the quarry. Were there more accidents prior to health and safety regulations or were there less risks taken?

The London to Holyhead A55 ran through the centre of Old Colwyn and Colwyn Bay and by the 1970s it proved to be inadequate for the volume of traffic and the size of many vehicles was causing concern over safety. A new bypass was proposed but it took many years for it to become a reality, eventually opening in the 1980s. As a result, much of Colwyn Bay and Old Colwyn were to be changed forever.

The railway goods yard near Colwyn Bay Station and the adjoining Pat Collins fairground were bulldozed through. Many houses and hotels were demolished. Major coastal defence work was begun from Old Colwyn to Llanddulas to enable the new expressway to be built safely out of reach of the highest tides. The railway line from Old Colwyn to Penmaenhead tunnel had to be moved to make room for the new road. Penmaenrhos Quarry had closed so it was convenient for the new expressway to run through it.

From the early years of the twentieth century Colwyn Bay had been a favourite holiday resort for many thousands of people from Liverpool, Manchester and the Midlands. They came in train loads for their annual summer holidays and would return year after year. Hotels and guest houses would be packed throughout the summer months, and many private houses kept visitors. Colwyn Bay, with its safe beaches and golden sands and its piers at Rhos-on-Sea and Colwyn Bay, its variety shows at the pavilion and many other attractions, was a busy seaside resort. Many people would visit out of season or come to rest or convalesce because of its pure air.

By the 1980s the tourist trade had declined very much owing to a number of factors. Many families by now had motor cars and would travel further afield for holidays. It was becoming easier to travel abroad and people were taking advantage of the offers being made by travel agents that were becoming popular. The advent of the A55 expressway did not help as motorists were now bypassing Colwyn Bay. The traditional summer holiday at a North Wales coastal resort now faced fierce competition. It was difficult to maintain hotels, guest houses and staff. Empty rooms would not pay bills. Overheads were high and the summer season was short leading to the hotels and guest houses having to diversify.

Like many seaside resorts Colwyn Bay proved to be a healthy, attractive and convenient place for retirement. Many who had holidayed here for many years chose to make it their place of retirement. Rhos-on-Sea drew a large number of Lancashire people who had been connected with the cotton mills. There were a high percentage of retired people in the area. Many in their later years could no longer cope in their large houses and were looking for somewhere smaller without the worry of gardens to care for. A number of the hotels were made into self-contained flats which were ideal for elderly people. There was a need for care homes and nursing homes; many hotels and guest houses diversified into this. Their rooms were full not just for summer trade but on a permanent basis. There was, however, a concern by some councillors that the area was drawing large numbers of elderly people from large towns and was in danger of being saturated with care and nursing homes. It was referred to at one time as 'Costa Geriatrica'.

Eventually new legislation was introduced and health and safety rules had to be observed. This made it difficult for many of these care homes to remain viable. Once again diversification was necessary. There was little choice apart from making flats or bedsits. This again led to a change in the population with an influx of people from outside the area. However this book is not an attempt to look at the social history of Colwyn Bay. Hopefully this will be done by someone to complement and update the works that have been published about the area in the past

It is now almost thirty years since I moved from Old Colwyn – what then is it that still inspires me to want to write or produce a book on the history of a place I have long since left? Through family and friends and local newspapers I have kept in regular contact and frequently visited. I still have the scrapbooks and newspaper cuttings I collected. The collection is much larger now as I have added many pictures and the collection is still growing. Many of the pictures in this book are from a personal collection and have never been published before.

During my childhood days in the 1950s the Borough of Colwyn Bay was made up of a number of smaller villages from the surrounding areas of Llysfaen and Penmaenrhos, Tan-y-Lan and Old Colwyn, Llanelian and Colwyn Bay, Rhos-on-Sea and Mochdre. Each of these 'villages' had its own identity, traditions and characters, which have long since disappeared. It is hoped this book will remind its readers of a time when these places were small and close-knit communities. Each village had its carnival which involved everyone. The sun always shone on carnival day and even if it did not, the rain never dampened the community spirit.

As a child I can remember how far Llysfaen seemed from Old Colwyn as it was a time when few families had motor cars. One could safely walk on a country lane and hear the sound of a car coming from a long way off. The chime of the St Catherine's church clock could be heard from most parts of Old Colwyn and on calm days at Old Colwyn it was possible to hear St Paul's church which is in the centre of Colwyn Bay.

Many of us never went away for a summer holiday. We did not need to. We had so much to do and enjoy at Colwyn. On a fine summer's day many families would take a bus ride to Eiria's Park. Here they could spend some time on the boating lake in a canoe or paddling boat, visit the café for a snack, play crazy golf, tennis or bowls, take a walk to the model-yacht lake, play hide-and-seek in the woods and rockery gardens, walk down to the promenade, take a ride on the miniature steam train to the pier or visit the Punch and Judy show. They may then walk slowly back along the promenade to Eirias Park purchasing ice creams at the kiosk to help us on our way. Sometimes we would take a trip on the promenade runabout bus to Rhos-on-Sea, spend the day at the outdoor swimming pool and maybe stay for a concert at the bandstand on the promenade in the evening.

I could happily write much more but this book is not meant to be an exhaustive account of my childhood memories. Rather, it is an attempt to record some of the pictures and places and events that have long since become lost in the mist of memories. I have tried to provide an accurate account of what is presented in this book. If any reader can correct any mistakes I may have made or give me any further information, which will be used if there is a revised edition in the future, I will be pleased to hear from you.

History is being made every day – maybe some of you have personal photos of groups of people or buildings or events. Please make an effort to record them with names, dates and places. Keep them safe or deposit them in the local archives. My experience from preparing this book is that so much of our local history has been lost.

Patrick Slattery
*November 2007*

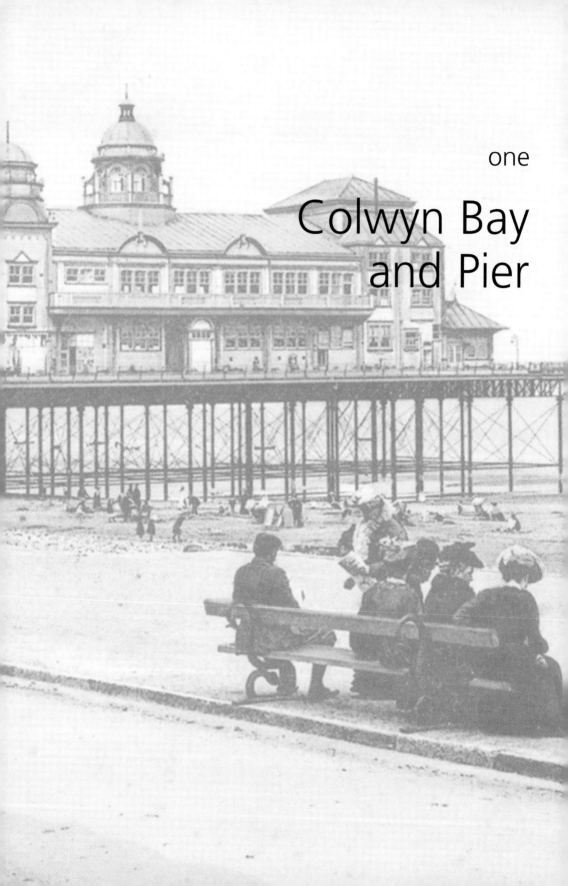

one

# Colwyn Bay
# and Pier

Colwyn is pretty well sheltered lying in a large sweeping bay between the headland of Penmaen Head and Rhos Point. It is surrounded by rolling hills which give much shelter to the area. It has been described as one of the most picturesque seaside resorts in North Wales. The panoramic view from Penmaen Head over the bay and round to Rhos Point is fascinating. With the arrival of the railway and the construction of a station, Colwyn Bay began to grow and become a very popular holiday resort. It was a favourite holiday spot for visitors from Liverpool, Manchester and the Midlands as it was easy to reach by train. Its safe beaches, golden sands, bracing air and surrounding hills enabled it to become one of the most popular seaside resorts of North Wales. It was unique as the railway was built on an embankment parallel to the sea from Penmaen Head to Colwyn Bay. The bay remains unspoiled as the promenade road which is adjacent to the railway embankment has left no room to build hotels or shops along the seafront.

It has been said there is only one view to equal that from Penmaen Head to Rhos-on-Sea and that is the view from Rhos-on-Sea to Penmaen Head. At low water the sands are a wonderful playground for children or an ideal spot for a nap in a deckchair. The steep railway embankment shelters the beach as it sweeps round to Penmaen Head. The hills steeply rise from Penmaen Head up to Llysfaen providing a natural shelter for the bay of Colwyn.

Sands and Pavilion.    Colwyn Bay.

By the end of the 1800s Colwyn Bay's popularity as a holiday resort was increasing and plans were made to construct a pier and pavilion. It was completed and opened in June 1900 and named in honour of Queen Victoria. The length of the Victoria Pier was 105 yards long.

PIER PAVILION, COLWYN BAY.

A grand pavilion was added to the Victoria Pier and could seat 2,500 people. Part of the pavilion housed a restaurant and there were shops each side of the main entrance. Madame Adelina Patti, known as 'the Queen of Song' was invited to sing at the opening concert. Crowds lined the street from the station to the pier to welcome her.

A forecourt was constructed to allow horses and carriages to draw up to the pier entrance. Two ticket offices were constructed with impressive domed roofs. Electric lighting was installed, and an orchestra was engaged and named Riviere's Grand Orchestra after its musical director Jules Riviere.

Because of its popularity the Victoria Pier was extended extensively to 350 yards. It was hoped to have a landing stage for pleasure steamers but this never materialized. The Bijou Theatre was constructed at the Pierhead. It seated 700 and held daily matinees and evening concerts. Daily concerts were held at the open air theatre near the pier. Minstrels and Pierrots entertained the visitors.

On a regular basis high tides and winter storms battered the pier and pavilion. Waves would crash upon the walls of the pavilion even up to its roof height. Amazingly very little damage was done as the pier and the pavilion were robustly constructed. Tragically the pavilion was gutted by fire in 1922.

A new pavilion was promptly constructed to replace the Victoria Pavilion. It was completed in 1923 and although it did not adopt the name of its predecessor 'The Victoria Pavilion' it was a very grand building. It was the venue of many popular shows and concerts. Because of the demand for entertainment a small theatre was constructed on the end of the pier. It was named the Alfresco Pavilion. Tragedy again came to the pier in 1933 when the Pier Pavilion was burnt down and later the Alfresco Pavilion was destroyed by fire.

Pier and Promenade, Colwyn Bay.

Despite losing two grand pavilions by fire in 1922 and 1933 the Colwyn Borough Council decided a pavilion was essential. Not only was it in use by tourists during the summer it was also frequently used to host many events during the winter months. A third pavilion was speedily constructed and opened in 1934. It was smaller than its predecessors yet could seat over 700. It also had a popular dance hall.

On fine sunny afternoons entertainment was provided from a bandstand on the pier. Deckchairs were provided for the audience to relax and enjoy the music. Youngsters could find entertainment on the golden sands where pony rides were popular.

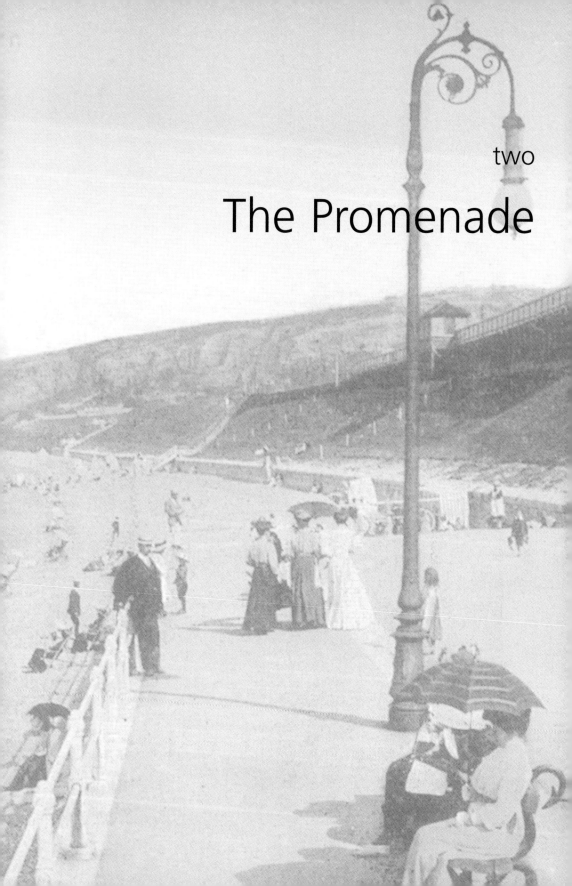

two

# The Promenade

The railway embankment was in danger of being eroded by stormy seas and Old Colwyn Station was in danger of collapsing as it was supported on stilts anchored into the embankment. A stone wall was built to protect the Old Colwyn Station and railway embankment.

Near to Colwyn Bay Station a large hotel was built around 1872 and appropriately named the Colwyn Bay Hotel. It was a landmark and could be seen miles away. There was need for a promenade to enable holidaymakers to have easy access to the beach. The first section was built near the hotel and a ramp was provided for boats. Because the promenade was much higher than the beach, safety railings were provided. The hotel was demolished in 1975 and replaced with a complex of retirement apartments named Princess Court.

THE PROMENADE & RHÔS-ON-SEA COLWYN BAY.

The beach was the property of the Crown and permission had to be granted prior to carrying out any work. The promenade was extended to Rhos-on-Sea, which was becoming a favourite place for tourists. For safety reasons, cast-iron railings were erected.

Eventually the promenade was extended east of the pier to Old Colwyn. Not only did this protect the railway embankment, it also made easy access to the beach at Old Colwyn. On completion it had enhanced the seafront. Visitors enjoyed a leisurely stroll along it and benches were situated to enable them to rest and enjoy the view and bracing air.

Electric light standards were erected around the pier. These proved to be so successful that in stages they were erected along the length of the promenade from Old Colwyn to Rhos-on-Sea. Eventually as electricity became more popular the whole of the promenade was illuminated and attracted many visitors at night time. The Cayley Promenade and embankment was a mass of coloured lights.

Crowds of visitors would walk up to Penmaen Head at dusk to see Colwyn Bay Promenade illuminations. The pier and its pavilion were also fully illuminated.

EAST PROMENADE, COLWYN BAY.

Promenade shelters were constructed and were welcome places to escape from blazing sunshine or a summer shower. Kiosks were provided where home-made lemonade and ginger beer, ice cream and sandwiches could be purchased. Motorists were beginning to discover Colwyn Bay and could park safely on its promenade road.

BEACH AND PROMENADE, OLD COLWYN.

Now the promenade was complete, the railway was fully protected but the sea wall took much battering. Groynes were erected along the beach to protect the sea wall from the force of the waves and the mighty winter storms. A slipway had been constructed at Old Colwyn to enable fishermen to bring their boats onto the beach.

*Promenade from Pier, Colwyn Bay*

A slipway was constructed to the east of the pier to enable Victorian bathing machines to be pushed onto the sands. These bathing machines were little wooden huts on wheels. The lady changed into her bathing costume in the hut, which was then wheeled down into the sea, where the she could descend the steps into the sea.

Some ladies would paddle along the water's edge as they were too shy to bathe. It would be difficult for them to hitch their long dresses up without revealing too much of their legs. Mixed bathing was allowed from 1901.

BEACH, PROMENADE & PENMAEN HEAD, OLD COLWYN.

A typical summer's day relaxing in a deck chair on the sands while the children made sandcastles or searched for crabs in the rock pools. At the end of the day the deckchair attendant stacked his chairs safely under the pier.

THE PROMENADE, GENERAL VIEW, COLWYN BAY.

Public conveniences were built to the west and east of the pier. A bandstand was constructed near the entrance to Eirias Park. It was the venue for brass-band concerts and various other artistes performed there.

A number of chalets were built on the embankment overlooking the beach to the east of Eirias Park entrance. They were ideal for the family to use and were often used by the same families year after year. Parents could keep an eye on their children as they played on the beach.

At the end of a long summer's day the happily tired and hungry holidaymakers would make tracks to their hotels or boarding houses for their evening meal.

Rough Sea, Promenade, Colwyn Bay.

Colwyn Bay had its share of storms during the winter months despite the bay being sheltered by the hills. Mighty waves would arise and crash against the sea wall with great force flinging up stones and shingle.

A ferocious storm in 1954 undermined a section of the sea wall near to the Eirias Park entrance. It also swept away the promenade road. Emergency repairs had to be carried out immediately as there was the danger of stormy seas sweeping further sections of the promenade away.

Rebuilding the sea wall and promenade was a very difficult task. Because of high tides it was only possible to work a few hours each day. This section being rebuilt is between Eirias Park entrance and Old Colwyn's 'Donkey Path'.

The work must be complete for the forthcoming summer season of 1954. Colwyn Bay had become a very busy tourist resort. It appealed very much to people from Manchester and the Midlands. This contractor's depot would have to be moved soon as it was at the entrance to Eirias Park which was a very popular place with tourists.

three

# Rhos-on-Sea

Rhos-on-Sea developed around the ancient church of Llandrillo-yn-Rhos which has connections with Ednyfed Fychan, a chieftain of the twelfth century. It is the earliest church in the Colwyn district and is looked upon as the mother church. It was a prominent landmark for sailors on the Irish Sea as they sailed to and from Liverpool. The cliff to the west of the church is the Little Orme and was quarried for limestone that was shipped to Liverpool and other ports to be used as road and building stone.

A road was built from Colwyn Bay to Rhos-on-Sea and it passed the front of Llandrillo church. Later the old stone rectory was demolished and a new rectory built to the right of the church. The original Ship Inn, built in 1736, was almost in front of The Rectory. It was demolished in 1874 and replaced the same year with a larger building named the Ship Hotel.

During the sixth century, St Trillo, a missionary monk from Breton, had settled at Rhos Point which became known as Rhos Fynach, meaning 'monk's promontory'. Rhos Fynach was one of the farms belonging to the Cistercian monks of Aberconwy. It was very near the sea and the monks based at Rhos Fynach had built a fishing weir on the beach built of large stones and stakes in a way so that fish were trapped in it at low tide.

THE ENTRANCE HALL
RHOS FYNACH, RHOS-ON-SEA

During the sixteenth century the Cistercian monks left and Rhos Fynach became part of the Lordship of Denbigh. It was later sold to a Captain Morgan who was an ancestor of Thomas Parry whose initials, and date (1717), are inscribed on a tablet on the exterior of Rhos Fynach. The interior remained unspoilt and had very low ceilings supported by oak beams. The ground floors consisted of large slate slabs. It was eventually purchased by Colwyn Council who wished to demolish it but it was listed as a building of historic interest. The council opened it as a café.

27

Rhos-on-Sea.

As Colwyn Bay became more popular as a holiday resort many visitors were attracted to Rhos-on-Sea. Doubtless the sweep of the bay and the fishing boats there were an attraction to many tourists. Before the promenade had been completed at Rhos-on-Sea many would walk along the beach to visit this little-known place.

Because of its splendid view over the bay and its healthy air a number of business people from Manchester and the Midlands would holiday at Rhos-on-Sea and eventually retire there. The cliff path was being eroded by the sea and plans were made to construct a sea wall and promenade as a continuation from the Colwyn Bay Promenade.

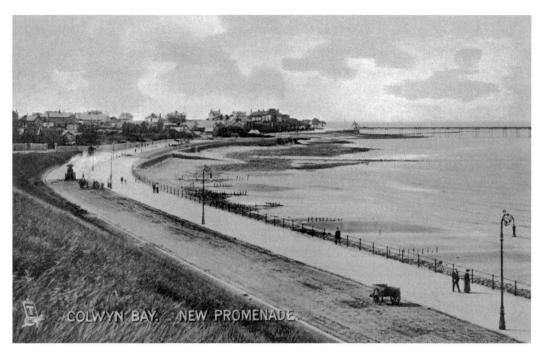

Here we see the completion of the new promenade to Rhos-on-Sea around 1909. Shelters were also constructed and electric lighting installed. Note the height of the cast-iron lighting columns to protect the lamps from shingle thrown up by rough seas.

The new promenade road to Rhos-on-Sea attracted more visitors and eventually a number of hotels were built. Colwyn Bay had entertainment on the pier and promenade. Now Rhos-on-Sea required entertainment. A bandstand was built on the Cayley embankment and later an open-air theatre where bands and orchestras would entertain the crowds on sunny afternoons.

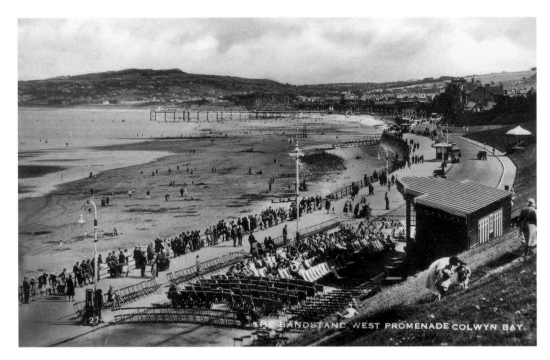

The open-air theatre became very popular and deckchairs were placed on the road to enable visitors to relax and enjoy the concerts. Traffic was diverted to the road above the theatre during concerts.

Rhos Pier can be seen to the centre right with its ticket office which still remains as part of a shop. The pier was bought second-hand from Douglas, Isle of Man where it had been constructed around 1890. It was opened during 1896 and its length was 1,240 yards. Pleasure steamers sailed from it to Liverpool and the Isle of Anglesey.

Rhos Pier never saw the glory of the Colwyn Bay Pier and its grand pavilion. Its lifespan was only some fifty-eight years. It was closed to the public during the Second World War. Much of the decking was removed for fear of any invading Germans landing there. Following the war it became very much neglected and lost its popularity. It required vast sums to be spent on it to bring it back to its glory and the decision to demolish it for safety reasons was made.

The remains of Rhos Pier during its sad ending by demolition in April 1954. The ticket office on the left of the picture still remains and is part of the shopping complex. On 20 July 1908 a pleasure steamer, the *Rhos Neigr*, hit rocks when trying to berth at the pier and sunk west of Rhos Point. The remains of the ship can still be seen at low tides.

Rhos promenade was soon developed with a number of large hotels. One of the most popular seafront hotels at Rhos-on-Sea was the Rhos Abbey, very near to the Rhos Pier. It had coaches and horses that collected visitors from Colwyn Bay Station.

Many visitors liked exploring the surrounding area and discovered that Bryn Euryn, a large hill (430ft) above Rhos-on-Sea, was a pleasant walk. On its slopes was the ruin of Llys Euryn, the home of Ednyfed Fychan, an ancestor through the Tudors of the present royal family. It is believed that long before the arrival of the Romans there was a fort on Bryn Euryn where the earliest inhabitants of Colwyn Bay settled.

From around 1840 limestone was quarried at Bryn Euryn and a railway constructed from it all the way down to Rhos seafront where a quay was built. Small sailing boats berthed here to be loaded with the limestone. The stone was taken to Liverpool and other ports to be used for buildings. A high-class hotel was built near to the quarry and called Tan y Bryn Hotel.

Colwyn Bay from Bryn Euryn

From the summit of Bryn Euryn on a clear day the Isle of Man, the Wicklow Hills and Blackpool Tower were visible. A panoramic view over Colwyn Bay following the coastline to Llanddulas, Abegele, Rhyl and Prestatyn made it a very popular walk for both visitors and residents.

*Above:* Looking west from near to Bryn Euryn over to Rhos-on-Sea, the new seaside resort, around 1890. The lengthy Rhos Pier (1,240 yards) can be seen here.

Trillo, a missionary monk from Breton in north-west France, settled at the Colwyn Bay area early in the sixth century. His task was to bring Christianity to Wales. His basic requirements for survival were fresh water and shelter. It is believed Trillo dug a well at this point and raised a shelter from mud and wattle over it. Eventually a stone chapel was built by the Cistercian monks and named St Trillo's chapel. It is the smallest church in Britain, seating six, and the well still remains under the tiny stone altar. The church is still in regular use.

Rhos-on-Sea eventually became a haven for yachting and a slipway was made near Aberhod for launching yachts. It became so popular that a sailing club was formed and still exists. On sunny summer afternoons the Bay of Colwyn would be a mass of white-sailed yachts.

An open-air swimming pool was constructed at Rhos-on-Sea at the rear of Rhos Fynach and Rhos Abbey Hotel. It was officially opened on 3 August 1933 by British boxing champion Jack Petersen. There was also a children's paddling pool above the main swimming pool. It was a very popular place on warm sunny days and drew large crowds. Gala and beauty competitions were also very popular. The large building to the left of the picture is the Rhos Abbey Hotel.

On warm, sunny days large crowds would come to the pool. There was something for everyone to do – swim, sit and watch, sunbathe or enjoy a snack in the café. There were often swimming galas and beauty competitions and weekly crazy nights. The temperature of the water was shown daily on a board and it is said by locals that several degrees were often added to the temperatures.

Rhos-on-Sea developed into a popular holiday resort and a retirement place. A number of shops and houses were built. Because they were almost at sea level they were often flooded when stormy seas crashed over the sea wall.

Firemen were always called out when flooding occurred as some of the cottages on the seafront were below sea level and the water had to be pumped away.

During 1982 a scheme was undertaken by the Colwyn Council to build a large stone barrier off Rhos Point which would prevent flooding. The stone was quarried at Penmon in Anglesey and brought by Dutch hopper barges to the site of the breakwater at Rhos Point.

Some stone was brought by lorry from a quarry at Ruthin in North Wales. It was tipped onto the beach at low water and hoisted onto the breakwater by large mechanical grabs. The contract was a lengthy one as work shifts were limited by the level of the tides.

The breakwater was completed in 1982 and put an end to the flooding. It also changed the nature of the beach by depositing tons of sand on top of the shingle. The breakwater also made it possible for many fishing and pleasure boats to moor safely on a permanent basis.

four

Around
Colwyn Bay

*Above:* Nant-Y-Hymon was one of the earliest houses on the outskirts of Colwyn Bay. These primitive dwellings were developed on common land between the seventeenth and nineteenth centuries. If a dwelling could be raised between dusk and dawn with smoke rising from its chimney the land was then claimed by them as freehold. The extent of the land was decided by how far the person could throw an axe from the four corners of the dwelling. Note the bowler-hatted gentleman leaning on the wall.

*Above:* Pwllycrochan Hotel was part of a large estate that had been the home of Sir David and Lady Erskine. The estate was sold in 1865 and became a hotel. A horse-drawn bus would carry visitors to and from the Colwyn Bay Station. It eventually became part of the nearby Rydal School.

*Right:* Pwllycrochan Woods became a popular spot for visitors to take walks and be shaded from the heat of the sunshine. A number of pathways were made through the woods, rustic bridges erected over streams and benches placed at various points.

RUSTIC BRIDGE, PWLLYCROCHAN WOODS COLWYN BAY.

*Opposite below:* A number of stone houses were built on Nant-Y-Glyn Road for farm workers and their families. This road led to the Old Highway which was the route to Upper Colwyn Bay and over to Llanrwst, a market town in the Conwy Valley.

Entrance to Nant-y-Glyn Valley, Colwyn Bay

The hills surrounding Colwyn Bay became popular haunts for visitors to walk and explore. They were not too far from the holiday resort and not too steep or difficult to walk. Footpaths were signposted and stiles erected in the Nant-Y-Glyn Valley to enable ramblers to enjoy the countryside above Colwyn Bay.

Plas-y-coed Colwyn Bay.

A number of Methodists from Manchester and the Midlands came regularly to Colwyn Bay for their holidays. They eventually developed Plas-y-Coed as the Methodist Guild Guest House. It was in a convenient spot near the Nant-Y-Glyn Methodist church. It attracted thousands of visitors annually but by the end of the 1980s could not compete with cheap continental holidays. It had a sad ending when it was gutted by fire and then demolished in 2002.

THE DINGLE, COLWYN BAY

*Above:* From Plas-y-Coed to the Eirias Park entrance from the promenade was The Dingle. It was a popular shaded walk along the side of the stream.

*Below:* This large building was known as the Hydropathic Establishment and opened in 1893 where people from the Midlands could come to rest and improve their health. Because of Colwyn Bay's mild climate and clean air it was a resort recommended by many doctors. It eventually became Penrhos College, a Wesleyan Methodist Boarding School for girls. It gained a reputation as a high-class college for girls and students from many parts of the world studied here. During the Second World War the entire college was evacuated to Chatsworth House in Derbyshire. The Ministry of Food took over the college and it did not reopen as a college till 1946. In 1975 it amalgamated with Rydal School in Colwyn Bay. The site was sold for residential development. The college was demolished and housing built.

*Above:* Colwyn Bay's Station Road led from the main road to Conwy down to the station. It was lined on both sides with trees and at its top was the Station Hotel which later became the Central Hotel. A large drinking fountain for horses was a prominent feature at the top of the road. This was removed in 1964 to allow easier access for traffic. On the corner opposite the station was the Imperial Hotel. Until the 1960s it was a very popular shopping street with high-class stores such as W.S. Woods and Daniel Allen's furniture store.

*Below:* Conwy Road became the main road from Old Colwyn to Conwy and Llandudno. It had a number of shops on each side and living accommodation above the shops. It was a pretty quiet road only used by horses and carts until the electric trams began to run from Llandudno in 1906.

Coed Pella Road, Colwyn Bay

Coed Pella Road led to the large Coed Pella Hotel and beyond to the Pwllycrochan Woods. Some of the large properties were used as offices. The *North Wales Weekly News* offices were in No. 5 and the Ministry of Labour Employment Exchange was housed in No. 7. Note the horse-drawn water tank and the man behind it clutching the water hose.

Looking down Coed Pella Road to Conwy Road 1958. On the left is a large building originally a pair of semi-detached houses that were bought by Colwyn Council in 1903 and made into council offices and a large extension added as a council chamber. The white-fronted building in the centre is Williams Deacons Bank and to the right the impressive red brick English Presbyterian church. Note the gas lamp; electric street lighting was not installed till the 1960s.

A fire broke out at Colwyn Bay Labour Exchange on Coed Pella Road in 1960. The front fire engine carries a tank of water and hoses. The rear one has the hydraulic ladder. The fire chief's van is parked on the left.

*Opposite above:* As the population of Colwyn Bay was increasing rapidly there was need for a new and larger administrative centre for the council. Glan y Don Hall, a magnificent building, was purchased and converted to make the imposing Civic Centre which was opened in May 1964.

*Opposite below:* Plas Bendith, the Theosophical Society's hall, in Coed Pella Road after a snowstorm in February 1955.

The Round Britain Cycle Tour passing through Colwyn Bay in 1953. Note the tram lines to the left of the cyclists and the large iron bracket supporting the overhead cables.

The Coed Pella Hotel eventually became the headquarters of the Colwyn Bay & District British Legion and was the venue for many military parades who would march from there to the War Memorial or St Paul's church for a service. This shows a British Legion Band assembling to march to the church for a dedication service in 1960.

The band awaits the parade marshal's command to begin the march.

The parade marches off to the church for a service to dedicate their new banners.

*Above:* The parade turns right onto Conwy Road and marches up to St Paul's church. Following the standard bearers are ex-servicemen who are members of the British Legion.

*Left:* Colwyn Bay was honoured to have a visit by Queen Elizabeth II as part of the Coronation celebrations on 19 July 1953. Great crowds had gathered to wave to the Queen. Note the hairdresser sign is above Tapp Smith the gents' hairdressers shop. A lone dog is waiting in the centre of the road to greet Her Majesty.

*Opposite above:* The crowds wave their banners and cheer as the Queen is driven slowly past. The royal car is escorted by a police car and followed by other dignitaries and royal staff.

*Opposite below:* An unfortunate accident on the new zebra crossing at Conwy Road. A learner driver on a motor scooter had lost control and swerved under the front of a lorry in 1959.

*Above:* The scooter was rescued from under the lorry and the police are now taking details as to how the accident happened. The police car is parked in front of the lorry and a police motor cycle by the motor scooter. The Mayfair was a high-class ladies' outfitters and Coopers a grocer's shop.

*Below:* This unfortunate accident occurred one night in 1959. The van hit a large tree outside Williams Deacons Bank at the junction with Coed Pella Road. The van belonged to Bartleys Stores, Nant Mawr Road, Buckley, fruiterers, florists & fishmongers.

Crowds line the main street in the centre of Colwyn Bay to see what was to be Colwyn Bay's largest wedding. Lord Colwyn's grandson was to marry his bride Miss Staveacre.

Lord Colwyn's grandson and his bride Miss Staveacre leaving St Paul's church, 1955.

*Left:* The bride, Miss Staveacre, arriving at the church on her father's arm 1955.

*Below:* A newly completed sea wall with built in benches was well used by visitors to sit and bask in the sunshine. August 1954.

five

Old Colwyn

The Old Village from Bridge, Old Colwyn

Old Colwyn developed around the Colwyn River which gave its name to the village. The building on top left was the first Wesleyan chapel at Colwyn. Below it was the slaughter house and a butcher's shop. The road led to the Colwyn Mill.

As Old Colwyn grew into a village, a road had to be constructed for access to and from Colwyn. It was part of the coaching route which developed into the London to Holyhead road. Old Colwyn was a watering and resting place and had five inns near to each other. To the left is the Ship Hotel entrance lamp. To the right is the Red Lion Hotel and to its left the Sun Inn. A tunnel had been constructed for the Colwyn stream to flow under the road. This picture was taken around 1910.

By 1908 electric trams ran from Llandudno to Colwyn Bay. The service was extended to Old Colwyn and to the Queens Hotel in 1915. The whitewashed cottages on the right were Plough Terrace, long since demolished for access to Rose Hill.

The Queen's Hotel was open in 1899 and named in honour of Queen Victoria. It had sixty bedrooms with splendid views over Colwyn Bay. It also had a tennis court in its grounds. During the Second World War like many of Colwyn Bay's hotels it was used by The Ministry of Food. The fields below it were part of Maes Cadwgan Farm and were needed to build on for a fast growing Old Colwyn. Station Road, Cadwgan Road, Wynnstay Road, Wynn Avenue and Wynne Drive are some of the roads found there today.

In 1906 Voryn Hall Holiday Camp was built on land between Queens Hotel and Penmaen Head. A number of chalets were constructed in its grounds. It was for many years a very popular holiday place. By the 1960s it lost popularity as many people were now going abroad for holidays.

The rocky headland that jutted out to sea at the east of Colwyn Bay was called Penmaen Head. Before the coach road was constructed it was mentioned by the Revd W. Bingley in his book, A Tour Round North Wales (1798) and by other travellers as being the most treacherous route on horseback between Holyhead and Chester. When the Penmaen Quarry was begun in the 1880s, some quarry workers' cottages were built on Penmaen Head and a large house erected called The Cliff for the manager of the quarry. Stone steps were constructed to enable quarry men to ascend and descend the cliff safely.

The quarry was worked out by 1963 and the Hotel Seventy Degrees was built on Penmaen Head. The builder was G.C. Jones of Llysfaen who had built the bungalows on Wynn Drive, Old Colwyn, and many other houses in the area. Hotel Seventy Degrees became a landmark and had one of the best views in North Wales. When the new A55 by pass was completed in the 1980s trade began to dwindle and eventually it was closed. It is to be demolished and replaced with residential housing.

The Penmaen Quarry along with the Llanddulas Quarries was one of the main industries in the area. During its lifespan of some eighty years the Penmaen headland that had jutted out to sea was quarried away. Hundreds of thousands of tons of limestone rock were taken from its jetty by boat to Liverpool and used to create a barrier to prevent the Mersey Docks silting up. Lots of stone went to Norway for use in the steel industry. Thousands of tons were shipped to Belgium for use in glass making. The large house near the left of the quarry face is The Cliff and to the right of it is Cliff Terrace. The fields above the quarry are now built upon. Note the quarry boat being loaded at the jetty. The access road to the quarry was very steep and winding and made it impossible to transport stone by road. It is remarkable that such a large amount of stone over the years was transported by sea.

The late Harold Thomas of Llanddulas who worked at Penmaen Quarry for many years. Helmets were supplied for quarry face workers and everyone wore hob nailed boots. The only protection from extreme weather would be a sack worn over the shoulders. The ship being loaded in the background is the *Turquoise*.

A familiar sight in the Bay of Colwyn was the number of quarry boats anchored daily awaiting high water so they could berth at the landing stages at the quarries to be loaded with limestone. The Penmaen and Llanddulas quarries were owned by Kneeshaw Lupton until 1922 when W. Robertson, the shipping line of Glasgow, purchased them. They had a number of coasters collectively called The Gem Line, named after semi-precious stones eg *Turquoise, Amber, Emerald, Pearl* and *Sapphire* and these were in permanent use to take the limestone from the quarries. They were painted black and red leaded up to the Plimsoll Line or loading line, the name on each side of the bow in large, gold letters. Raynes Quarry at Llanddulas was bought by ICI who had their own coasters painted battleship grey and named after chemicals eg *Calcium, Thorium, Sodium, and Barium*. During summer holidays large crowds would gather to watch quarry boats coming to load at the jetties.

The Penmaen Quarry was worked out in 1963 as it had almost reached the wall of the railway tunnel. The men transferred to the Llanddulas Quarry. One of the last boats to be loaded there was the 3,000 ton *Emerald*. It took three hours to load its three hatches.

The quarry mill and crusher and jetty were demolished in 1964 and it became a dumping ground for builders waste and scrap cars. Plans for a badly needed Colwyn Bay bypass were in the pipeline and it began in the 1980s. The route would take it right through the centre of the quarry. Here we see the work proceeding and the bow bridge being erected in 1982.

By 1983 the bypass was opened and although it had solved the traffic problems it also had a devastating effect on tourism to the area. This picture shows the expressway running through the Penmaen Quarry.

The only building the demolition gang failed to remove from the quarry was this concrete gunpowder store. It had a stone wall surrounding it but that was removed along with its exterior iron door. The interior was lined with pitch pine panels. Before entering the building (known as a 'Magazine'), hob-nailed boots had to be removed and 'magazine slippers' put on. Harry Foulkes was the 'Blaster' up to the time the quarry closed in 1963. He had to prepare fuses, gunpowder and detonators for the daily blasting.

The Chester & Holyhead Railway Co. began to construct the line in the 1840s. It meant constructing many viaducts and tunnels as it crossed valleys. The Penmaen Head tunnel was one of the most difficult as caves penetrated it making much more masonry strengthening work necessary. It was completed around 1847. Here we see a British Rail Standard 73021 with 'down' express leaving Penmaen Tunnel on its way to Llandudno, 1953.

Old Colwyn Station platform was propped up on wooden stilts anchored into the embankment. Owing to the proximity of the station day trippers did not have far to walk to the seashore. This picture was taken in 1909.

The Old Colwyn Railway Viaduct completed around 1847 was one of several on the Chester to Holyhead route. Within a mile of this a similar one had to be constructed at the Eirias Park entrance. The semi-detached cottages known as Glan y Mor were often flooded as no sea wall had been constructed as yet. Mary and Edward Williams lived in the right hand one and brought up eight children there. Mary kept a tiny wooden shop nearby and sold home-made ice cream in the summer. It was kept cool in a container in a hole in the ground.

*Above:* The road from Old Colwyn village centre to the beach followed the Colwyn River. It was called Beach Road. Tan-y-Coed Gardens and mansion was built by a Manchester business man Sir Charles Woodall around 1875. He later built Glanaber and its stables on the opposite side of the Colwyn River. His gardener and other staff lived here. He was fond of smoking a pipe but not allowed to smoke in the house. He built the Tower Folly on the highest point of Tan-y-Coed Gardens and used it as a place where he could enjoy his pipe. After his death Colwyn Council purchased the estate. It was opened as a tea garden in the summer.

*Below:* Tan-y-Coed Gardens were looked after for many years by the late Norman Roberts and Glyn Williams who were employed by Colwyn Council. They also looked after Min-y-Don Park, Fairy Glen, Wynn Gardens and Cliff Gardens. The gardens were always kept tidy, well stocked and cultivated and were a credit to Old Colwyn. The picture shows the Tower Folly and to its left St Augustine's Priory and the Sefton Hotel.

The view of Old Colwyn from St John's church tower, 1920. The road on the left, Station Road, leads to Old Colwyn Station and the road on the right is Beach Road. The fields on the left stretch up to Llanelian and to the right Nant-y-Glyn Valley.

Not far from Old Colwyn Station were the Endsleigh Boarding houses seen in centre of picture. To the left is Sefton Road and its row of boarding houses. To the right of the picture above the haystack can be seen houses on Queens Road which led from the Queens Hotel down to Old Colwyn Station.

Through the Fields to Penmaen. *Old Colwyn.*

Before the Tan-y-Lan Estate had been built fields stretched from the foot of Penmaen Head down to the beach. There was a footpath to Penmaen which went through Uwch-y-Don Farm fields. To the top left of the picture is Bay View and below it Eirias Terrace on Miners Lane. On the extreme right the large building is Arvon House. It became D.O. Roberts, butchers and Mrs Percival, newsagent.

Promenade and Penmaen Head, Old Colwyn

A leisurely stroll along the promenade to Old Colwyn on a summer's afternoon early 1900s. Old Colwyn Station can be seen centre left. The Penmaen Quarry and jetty can be seen in the distance. The road led under the magnificent limestone railway viaduct to Beach Road and Old Colwyn village.

Penmaen Head, Old Colwyn.

Many visitors would walk to look at Penmaen Head and Quarry. This picture is of Rock Cottage, a smallholding where the Nolan family had lived for many years. The steam train is approaching the tunnel. To the left of the tunnel is Tan-yr-Ywen, a row of quarry workers cottages.

Tan-y-Tip cottage was near the quarry entrance and believed to be one of the first cottages to be built. It had a reed and turf roof. Water was drawn from a nearby spring.

The Penmaen Quarry jetty was a landmark and from the 1880s to 1963 was used several times a week to load steam-hopper barges with limestone and later some very large coasters. Initially trucks were pulled along the jetty by cable to be emptied into hopper barges. Eventually a conveyor belt operated by a diesel engine was installed. The jetty was constructed of greenheart which was as hard as iron. The quarry canteen was to the right of the jetty and the crushing plant and hoppers for storing stone are seen above the canteen.

Caves and Penmaen Head, Old Colwyn

The beach from the jetty to Llanddulas was very rocky. These caves were part of a large number that had gone very far into Penmaen Head. When the railway tunnel was being constructed it experienced problems of breaking into caves which meant a lot of filling and strengthening of the tunnel walls.

The view from Penmaen Quarry looking east to the Llanddulas Quarries . The steamer in the foreground is at Raynes Quarry jetty. Beyond are two further jetties belonging to Kneshaw Lupton's Quarry.

Cliff Gardens was a pleasant place to sit and relax or shelter from the sunshine on a summer's day. Along with the nearby promenade it was illuminated at night time during the summer months. This picture shows Colwyn's last Victorian shelter, demolished in 1980.

When the new A55 Colwyn bypass was constructed, Cliff Gardens was bulldozed along with part of Min-y-Don Avenue and Station Road. Reinforced concrete columns were raised in front of the railway viaduct in preparation to carry the new road.

The new expressway meant a lot of housing was demolished. This picture from Penmaen Head looking down at Old Colwyn shows the railway to the right. To the left of the railway is Tan Lan Crescent which were homes for the elderly. These were demolished along with Tan Lan Post Office and Eskdale Stores, Marine Road and Roseberry Avenue.

The expressway followed the landward side of the railway line to Penmaen Head tunnel. It was then routed to go through the old Penmaen Quarry. This caused a major problem meaning the railway line would have to be moved onto a temporary embankment and a railway viaduct erected alongside it to enable the road to cross to the seaward side of the railway and on into the old quarry. This picture is of the new railway viaduct before excavating for the road to cross to the seaward side underneath it. The hotel Seventy Degrees is the building seen at the top of Penmaen Head.

The completed railway viaduct 1992. The road runs under it to the seaward side and into the old Penmaen Quarry.

*Above:* This picture shows the completed expressway in 1993. This section caused a massive problem as it was nearing Penmaen Railway tunnel. The road had to be taken through the Penmaen Quarry. To enable this to happen the railway line had to be moved onto a temporary embankment and a viaduct had to be constructed for the road to run under the railway and into the old quarry.

*Below:* A reinforced concrete retaining wall had to be constructed in front of the houses on Tan Lan Road and a concrete pedestrian bridge for access to the beach.

The foundation of the expressway as it leaves the Penmaen Quarry for Llanddulas. The ICI quarry jetty had to be demolished and a new one built.

The newly constructed ICI landing stage with a boat being loaded. Hundreds of thousands of reinforced concrete anchors were cast and placed along the seashore from Penmaen Quarry to Llanddulas to prevent rough seas eroding the new expressway.

The expressway passes alongside the Llanddulas Quarry. A small tunnel was constructed to enable the conveyor belt from the quarry to go under the road and on to the jetty.

Old Colwyn had some very pleasant walks and one of the most popular was the Fairy Glen which was a lovely wooded walk alongside the Colwyn stream.

The rustic bridge over the Fairy Glen waterfall led to the Old Colwyn Mill and Pen-y-Bryn.

Wynn Gardens was a popular spot for spending a relaxing hour. The flower beds and shrubs and lawns were always well kept. Wynn Gardens is situated between Wynn Avenue and Wynnstay Road and nearby is the imposing Queens Hotel.

Beyond the Queens Hotel was Gorphwysfa, which became a girls' boarding school. It had extensive grounds where the girls could exercise.

Next to Gorphwysfa was the Uwch-y-Don Hall and Farm. The land was sold for building purposes and in 1933 the hall was converted into a home for blind children from Manchester and renamed the White Heather Home. It eventually closed in the 1970s, demolished and Rhos Gwyn flats have replaced it. The impressive building can be seen in the foreground of this picture. Behind it are the Endsleigh Road boarding houses.

*View from Golf Links, Old Colwyn*

A much favoured place was the Old Colwyn Golf Links with its nine-hole golf course and spectacular views for miles around. This picture taken from the links looks over to Plas Parciau and farm on the left. To the right is Min Afon and its farm buildings. The hills are part of upper Colwyn Bay.

BEACH ROAD, OLD COLWYN.

Beach Road was one of the busiest roads during the summer time as residents and visitors made their way to and from the beach. St John's church tower is prominent in this picture taken in the early 1900s.

Maes-y-Coed was on the outskirts of Old Colwyn village was a home for elderly members of Bethesda Wesleyan chapel. Its extensive grounds were sold off for building the Maes-y-Coed Estate.

Maes-y-Coed was sold in the 1980s and Deakin electrical engineers built their new premises on the site. They sold the premises to Bethel Pentecostal church which moved from their building on the opposite side of the road. It is now Bethel Community church.

At a public meeting held in Colwyn Bay in 1897 it was decided to commemorate the Diamond Jubilee of Queen Victoria by building a hospital. As a result Colwyn Bay Cottage Hospital was built by public subscription in 1898 on Hesketh Road between Old Colwyn and Colwyn Bay. It was extended in 1925 and over the years has been modernised and kept to a high standard. It is now known as the Colwyn Bay Community Hospital.

Old Colwyn village had a number of small but high-class shops which catered for everyone's needs. Treleavens Prize Bakery was a very well known family business on the corner of Princess Road.

Treleavens delivered bread, confectionery and groceries to many of the outlying farms and villages by horse and cart. Eventually two vans were purchased for deliveries. Frank Treleaven Jones is in the centre with the dark hat with Tom Jones and Emlyn Evans.

Old Colwyn shopping centre in the 1950s. The car is turning into the rear of the Plough Hotel. The building on the left is the District Bank. The trams had disappeared but the iron column for the overhead cable remains and is used as a street light.

Looking up Colwyn's main street, *c.* 1900. Plough Terrace on the left was a row of six tiny cottages. The poster on the wall is advertising the English Wesleyan chapel's preachers for the next Sunday as Mr T. Schofield and James Feather, 'A Hearty Welcome To All. All Seats Are free'. The large building at the centre is the premises of Evan Roberts, butcher who had a slaughter house at the rear.

Min-y-Don Hall, 1906, originally Colwyn Farm and dating back to the 1700s became the home of Hugh Clough a descendant of Sir Richard Clough of Denbigh. It became a boys' school around 1900 and was demolished in 1938. The stable block remains and was made into a house called Cwrt Bach. This picture of boys and staff outside the hall was taken in 1905.

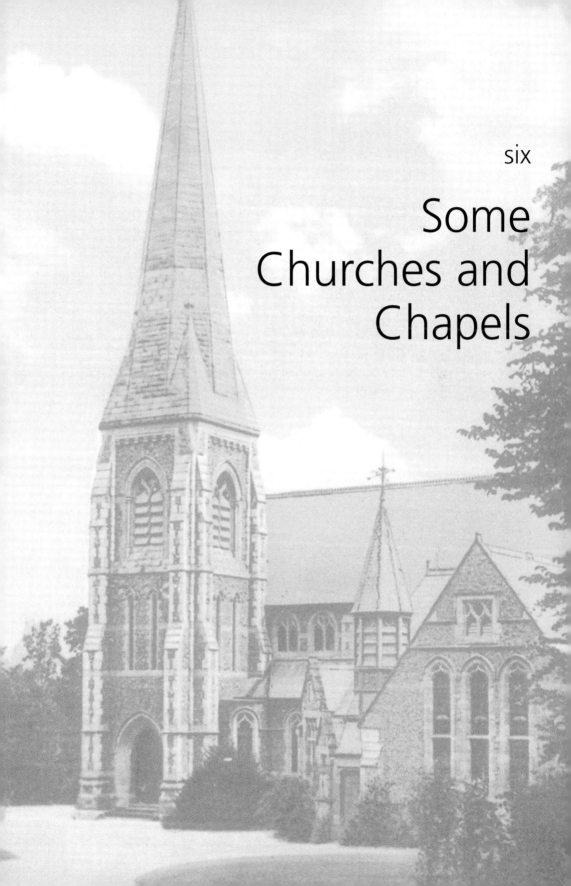

six

# Some
# Churches and
# Chapels

*Above:* Llandrillo-yn-Rhos is the mother church of the area. It dates back to at least the twelfth century and is believed to have been built by Ednyfed Fychan, a Welsh chieftain.

*Below:* St Paul's church is an impressive building in the centre of Colwyn Bay. It was built on land donated by Sir Thomas Erskine of the Pwllycrochan Estate. The present building opened in 1888 but the chancel was not built until 1895. A large vicarage was built to the right of the church.

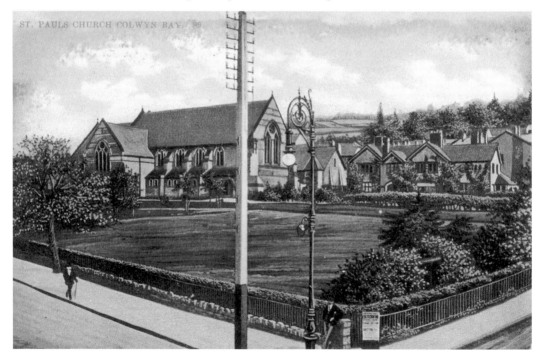

45965. COLWYN BAY: ST. PAUL'S CHURCH.

*Above:* A tower with a clock on four sides was added to the church in 1911. A much smaller church for Welsh language services was built behind St Paul's in 1903 and named St David's. The main road through Colwyn Bay can be seen to the left.

*Below:* Due to its convenient location in the town centre, St Paul's has always been used by various organisations such as the annual Remembrance Day services and Mayor's Sundays. It can also accommodate for large numbers and is a well-lit building with good acoustics. It has always been popular for weddings.

INTERIOR OF ST. PAUL'S CHURCH, COLWYN BAY

*Above:* Bryn-y-Maen church in the hamlet among the hills above Colwyn Bay is known as the 'Cathedral in the hills'. Tourists were often surprised to see such a large impressive building in such a small hamlet. It was designed by John Douglas of Chester who had designed St Paul's church, Colwyn Bay. It was dedicated in 1897 in memory of Charles Frost a wealthy landowner. His wife Eleanor donated the money in memory of him.

*Left:* St John's English Methodist church was begun in 1882 by the Revd Frederick Payne when the foundation stone was laid. Because funds were not being raised as well as planned, the building was left uncompleted for some years and called 'Wesley's Folly'. Eventually funds were raised and the impressive building was opened in 1888.

COLWYN BAY: ST. JOSEPH'S CATHOLIC CHURCH

To meet the spiritual requirements of tourists and a number of retired people who had moved to Colwyn Bay a Catholic church was required. In 1895 a Catholic priest was based in Colwyn Bay and services held in a house in Rhiw Road. Eventually a piece of land was bought to the west of St John's and the Catholic church was built there and completed in 1900. By 1933 a Catholic school was built behind the church and run by the Sisters of Mercy.

In the hills above Old Colwyn is the hamlet of Llanelian-yn-Rhos. It was famed for many years for its cursing well. The ancient church was founded around 540 AD, originally a wattle-and-daub building. Centuries later the stone building was raised. Parts of the existing building are believed to date to the ninth century. It is unique as to enter the church one has to go through the forecourt of the White Lion inn.

Old Colwyn was part of Llandrillo-yn-Rhos Parish and St Catherine's church was built as a chapel of ease in 1837. The land was donated by John Wynn of Coed Coch Estate. By 1844 Old Colwyn became a parish and St Catherine's the parish church. It seated 250 and 156 seats were for the poor of the parish. The tower clock was installed in memory of the Revd J.D. Jones vicar from 1866-1887. A large vicarage was built opposite in 1871 which was sold in the 1980s and Llys Madoc flats built in the grounds.

St John's church on Station Road, Old Colwyn was begun in 1899 when the foundation stone was laid by Mrs Eleanor Frost of Min-y-Don who was a great benefactor to the church. The church was open on 13 August 1903 at a cost of £12,300.

*Above:* St John's church tower was an addition to the building in 1912 at a cost of £2,300. Mr Charles Howe and his sister Miss Howe, donated £1,000 in memory of their parents towards the building the tower. Mr Howe was a businessman who lived at The Haven, Wynn Avenue. The family were great benefactors of the church.

*Below:* The interior of St John's church was greatly enhanced by the goodwill and generosity of many influential Colwyn people. The pipe organ was donated in 1903 by Mrs Cornelia Bagnall of Colwyn House in memory of her aunt.

ADRODDIAD
BLYNYDDOL

Eglwys yr Annibynwyr

" EBENEZER," COLWYN

Am y Flwyddyn 1964

J. H. WILLIAMS (ARGRAFFWYR) CYF., ABERGELE

Ebenezer Welsh Congregational church is the oldest church in Old Colwyn. Its beginnings go back to 1804 when the Revd Azariah Shadrach of Llanrwst came to preach at Nant chapel, Llanelian. He was persuaded to preach at Old Colwyn in Bryn-y-Gwynt cottage. From then on services were held for eleven years at Bryn-y-Gwynt and numbers grew too large to meet in the house. Land was bought on the main route through Colwyn on the corner of Albert Road, a small chapel built and opened in 1815. Its numbers increased and it had to be altered in 1848 and extended in 1860. The membership was steadily increasing as Colwyn was growing and major alterations were carried out in 1881. In 1904 a pipe organ was installed at a cost of £150. A schoolroom was built alongside the chapel in 1899. The annual report for 1964 shows Ebenezer chapel as it was from 1881 and it remains unchanged. The Revd W.E. Penllyn Jones, who was a renowned bard and won over a dozen chairs at Eisteddfodau, was minister from 1880-1922. He composed many hymns and was a well-known historian.

*Left:* The Llystaen Wesleyans had built a small chapel on Bwlch-y-Gwynt Road in 1803 on land bought from Bryniau Cochion farm. Its membership eventually made the building too small so a large piece of land was donated by William Arthur Foulkes of Fron Felen Farm on Tan-y-Graig Road. A new chapel was built in 1906 and named Mynydd Seion. It had seating for over 200. The stone was quarried locally near to the Castle Inn. The farm buildings were behind the chapel and haystacks alongside it.

*Opposite above:* Old Colwyn English Congregational church began in 1898 in Ebenezer Welsh Congregational schoolroom. A suitable piece of land became available next to Min-y-Don Park and was bought. The church was built and opened in 1925. A large hall was erected at the rear and used for plays and pantomimes and concerts. The hall is now used by MASE (Music and Sound Experience), a recently formed charity to enable people to explore their creativity through music and experience.

*Below:* Old Colwyn English Baptist church had its beginnings in the home of a Mrs Esther Parry in Pen-y-Bryn. Services were held from 1885 until 1891. The numbers increased and a strip of land was bought and a 'tin chapel' made from a second-hand building was purchased. The building was too small for the growing congregation and there was no room to extend. Land was bought on the corner of Princess Road and the present church built and opened in 1906 at a cost of £2,500.

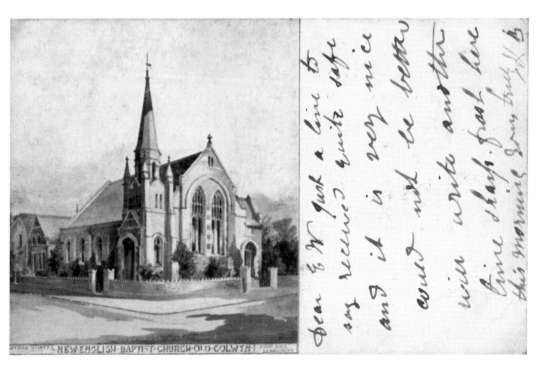

Old Colwyn English Baptist church on Princess Road. The appearance of the building has not changed since it opened in 1906.

The first Calvinistic Methodist chapel at Old Colwyn was built at Rose Hill in 1861 and called Hebron. The terraced houses built alongside it were called Hebron Terrace. By the end of the 1800s Hebron was too small for the growing congregation so it was made into a house. A strip of land was bought on the Penmaen side of Old Colwyn at the junction of Bodelwyddan Avenue. A large chapel and schoolroom were erected and open in 1904.

*Above:* The exterior appearance of Hebron chapel has scarcely changed in over 100 years. Internally it has been altered – the ceiling was in a dangerous state and was replaced with a false ceiling in the 1980s.

*Right:* The Annual Report for Hebron chapel, Colwyn 1967, shows how well supported the church was. The minister at the time was late Revd John Wynn Williams who was instrumental in helping two of the Sunday school members to become ministers – David Andrew Jones of Clobryn Farm and Glyn Tudwal Jones of Old Colwyn. Both are Presbyterian ministers now serving at Cardiff. The minister was assisted by a number of elders. Membership for 1967 was 273 plus a Sunday school of sixty-three children.

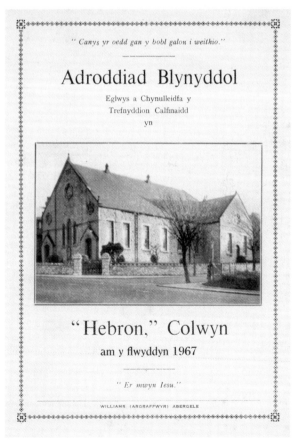

" *Canys yr oedd gan y bobl galon i weithio.*"

## Adroddiad Blynyddol

Eglwys a Chynulleidfa y
Trefnyddion Calfinaidd
yn

"Hebron," Colwyn

am y flwyddyn 1967

" *Er mwyn Iesu.*"

WILLIAMS (ARGRAFFWYR) ABERGELE

The Welsh Baptists of Old Colwyn began in a small chapel at the top of Church Walks in 1862. As the premises became too small for the growing congregation, a new building was erected in 1863 on Princess Road at a cost of £1,860. It had a baptistry under the floor in front of the pulpit.

*Opposite above:* A Sunday school trip from Calfaria Baptist chapel in the early 1900s. It was an era when hats and caps were very fashionable. The driver of the coach wearing a peaked cap is standing on the far right.

*Opposite below:* The first Welsh Wesleyan Methodist chapel at Old Colwyn was built at Pen-y-Bryn in 1832 and called Bethesda. It opened on Christmas day 1832 and preaching services were held at 5 a.m., 10 a.m., 2 p.m. and 6 p.m. It became inadequate for the growing congregation and a new one was built on the main road in 1886. When it closed part of it was used as a warehouse and part as a house still called Bethesda House.

*Above:* The interior of the new Bethesda chapel. The pipe organ was installed in 1925 at a cost of £1,125. The minister, the Revd W.O. Evans, and trustees Mr Robert Evans of 'Mohcroft', Meiriadog Road and Mr Ellis Jones gave opening speeches. An organ recital was given by Dr Caradog Roberts of Rhosllanerchrugog.

*Left:* Harvest decorations around the pulpit area of Bethesda chapel before the pipe organ was installed in 1925.

*Opposite:* The centenary celebration booklet of 1932 showing the new Bethesda chapel, built on Old Colwyn's main street in 1886. The stone was from a local quarry and transported free of charge by horse and cart. This was by the goodwill of Mrs William Jones of Ty Newydd Farm who owned a haulage business. Her son Robert paid for much of the stone.

# Yr Eglwys Fethodistaidd, Colwyn
## CANMLWYDDIANT

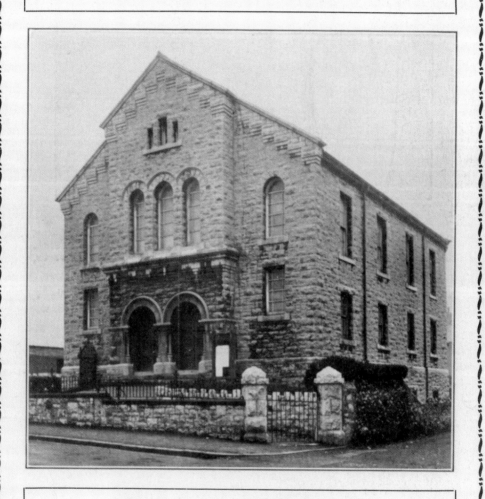

# BETHESDA
## 1832 = 1932

*Above:* Bethesda chapel, Colwyn, 150th anniversary celebrations, December 1982. Left to right: Revd Lewis Valentine (retired Baptist minister), Revd Selwyn Closs Parry (Vicar of Colwyn), Revd John Davis (St John's Methodist church, Colwyn Bay), Revd J. Wynn Williams, (Hebron), Revd Dr O.E. Evans (Llanfair P.G – guest preacher), Revd J. Haines Davies (minister of Bethesda from 1970).

*Opposite above:* Bethesda 150th anniversary celebrations December 1982. Some of the members who took part in a play called 'Thomas Coke'. Left to right: Mr Edmund Jones, Mrs Mair Jones, Mr Ben Thomas, Mr Martin Blythin.

*Opposite below:* Disgwylfa chapel, Penmaenrhos opened in 1901 as a branch of Bethesda chapel. It was built by Mr Robert Evans of Bay View, the house to the left of the chapel. The stone was from the nearby quarry and many local men helped with the building. The total cost for land and building was £527.

Disgwylfa annual coffee evening with bring and buy stall outside the chapel in 1978.

Bethel Welsh Congregational church on Miners Lane was opened in 1881. The builder was Mr J.W. Vaughan of Colwyn. The cost of the land and building plus a caretaker's house was only £248. A road widening scheme in 1937 meant the chapel had to be demolished.

The new Bethel chapel built on a new site on Miners Lane. Membership has declined but it is still used and some English services are also held.

Old Colwyn's English Methodist church on Wynn Avenue was built in 1909. It became known as Coy's church because Mr Alfred Coy and his wife pioneered much of the work that was carried out by the church.

The Sunday school drew large numbers of children throughout the years and had a popular youth club. This picture is of the Old Colwyn English Methodist Sunday school, 1980.

Old Colwyn Catholic church began here in St Augustine's Priory in 1933. The mother superior allowed Catholic visitors to use the Convent chapel. In 1956 a Catholic church was built to the left of the Convent. It was named the church of the Sacred Heart.

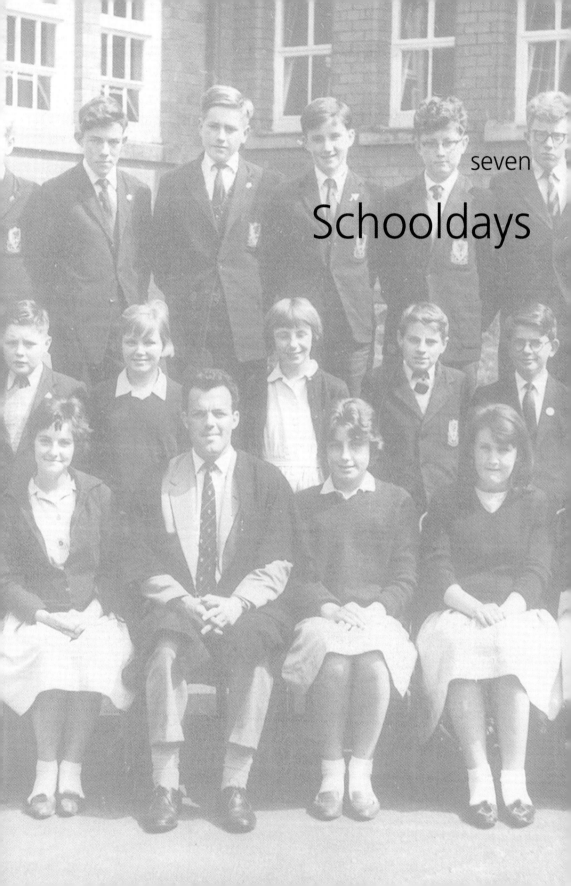

seven

# Schooldays

Old Colwyn County Junior Mixed School. Miss Cole's Class, 1958. Back row, from left to right: Timothy Spence, Graham Lloyd Jones, John Davies, Stuart Bowden, Michael Vaughan, Roger Roughley, Peter Herron, Michael Norris, Morgan Howes, Roberts, Patrick Slattery. Second row: Carol Walker, Susan Roberts, Heather Scott, Catherine Jones, Judith Waterworth, Roberta Worthington, Gwyneth Jones, Lynette Protheroe, Glyn Tudwal Jones. Third row: Adrian Miller, Glenys Roberts, Lynda Jenks, Claire Hannah, Jennifer Jones, Pamela Hughes, Christine Edwards, Carol Jones, Lilian Roberts, Susan Murell. Seated: Philip Davies, Kelvin Owen, Jonathan Clarke, Christopher Brewerton, Geoffrey Davies, David Humphreys, Emlyn Crossley, William Eyre.

*Opposite above:* Old Colwyn County Junior Mixed School in Church Walks was opened in the 1931and had nine classrooms. Three were for the infants and six for the juniors. It also had a large hall which was used for assemblies and concerts and as the school dining hall. There were separate entrances for boys and girls and also separate playgrounds.

*Opposite below:* Colwyn Bay Grammar School in 1960 before the new extension was added. It was opened in 1903 as the Higher Grade School, situated on Dingle Hill, and is now on the edge of Eirias Park. By 1923 numbers of pupils increased and two rows of wooden huts were used as classrooms and positioned at the rear of the school. They were used until 1969. It became a comprehensive school in 1967 and was combined with the Pendorlan Secondary School and renamed Colwyn High School.

Colwyn Bay Grammar Form 2C, June 1962. Back row, from left to right: Michael Townsend, Michael Bacon, John Swain, Clive Homan, Roger Bolton, Glyn Tudwal Jones, Alun Griffiths, Ian Wood, Philip Davies. Centre; Michael Edwards, Brian Davies, Jonathan Hughes, David Haygreen, Gareth Roberts, Patrick Slattery, Geoffrey Davies. Front row: Lynne Whittingham, Kathryn Bryan Williams, Anita Williams, Christine Little, Mr Ralph Dicken (form master), Lynn Randerson, Roberta Worthington, Janis Hughes, Sandra Williams.

# eight

# Transport

The main road link from Colwyn to Llandudno was mainly used by horses and carts up to the arrival of the trams in 1907. The trams initially ran from Llandudno to Rhos-on-Sea where there was a tram depot in Penrhyn Avenue. The service was then extended to Colwyn Bay and because of its popularity again extended in 1915 to Queen's Hotel Colwyn. This picture shows a tram passing Colwyn Bay's Central Hotel in 1912.

Llandudno and Colwyn Bay Electric Tramways Co. showing tramcar No. 12 at the Colwyn Bay terminus at the junction to Greenfield Road with passengers boarding for Llandudno. This picture was taken prior to the extension of the tram service to Old Colwyn in 1915.

CLIFF ROAD, OLD COLWYN                                        219683 ②

Most visitors arrived by train and holiday specials would arrive daily during the high season. This holiday special from Manchester crossing Old Colwyn viaduct for Colwyn Bay Station.

By the 1950s the trams were replaced with motor buses. The company had a fleet of red and cream buses that ran from Llandudno to Colwyn Bay. There was competition from the Crosville Bus Service which had provided a much used service all over the Borough of Colwyn Bay.

Crosville's green and cream double-decker service No. 408, Colwyn Bay to Llandudno, at Colwyn Bay town centre in the 1950s.

Colwyn Council ran a fleet of Runabout Buses throughout the summer season. They began at Old Colwyn Promenade and terminated at Rhos Point. Later a service was provided to Eirias Park and the Welsh Mountain Zoo.

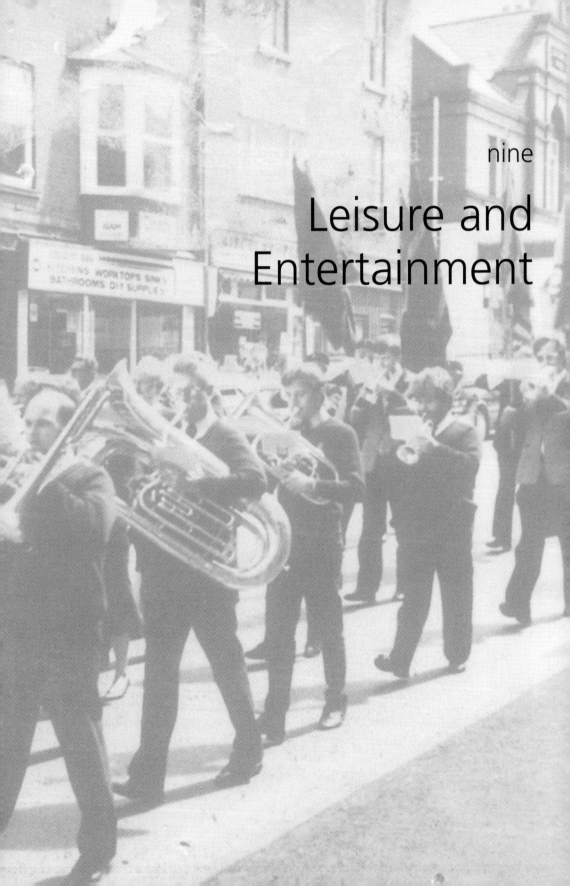

nine

# Leisure and Entertainment

Eirias Park had something for all ages from golf to tennis, canoes and model boating, concerts and cafes, wooded walks and rock gardens. This picture is of Don Pedros Band giving a concert at Eirias Park in 1927.

The model yachting pond at Eirias Park where adults and children could safely sail and race their model yachts and boats.

*Above:* The Boating Lake at Eirias Park, *c.* 1939. Canoes or paddle boats could be hired. Parents would sit on the benches around the lake and relax in the sunshine watching their children on the lake. During the winter months the lake was drained and children would go hunting in the mud for newts and lizards.

*Below:* An arson attack on the boat house and its thatched roof at Eirias Park in 1978. All that is left are the concrete supports and iron girders.

The rock gardens and railway viaduct at Eirias Park in the 1950s.

A miniature steam railway ran between the promenade road and railway embankment. It started by the pier and terminated at the Dingle Halt which is the entrance to Eirias Park.

During the 1960s the Colwyn Council provided this Welsh Ffargo Express service from Colwyn Bay Pier along the promenade to The Dingle and up the steep hill to Eirias Park Café.

Colwyn Bay Carnival was an event that was very popular. This picture taken in 1930 shows the parade passing Greenfield Road on its way to Eirias Park. The boy scouts leading are; front: Dick Slattery of Fairmount, Old Colwyn and second left Evan Davies of Beach Road, Old Colwyn. The decorated name above the gondola says 'Vera' who was the carnival queen.

*Above:* Colwyn Town Band led many carnivals and other processions. Here we see it heading the Mayor's Sunday Parade in 1988.

*Left:* Colwyn Band awaiting for the parade marshal to shout 'By the left quick march' at Mochdre Carnival 1966. The young tenor horn player on the left is Patrick Slattery and on the right with the tuba is Arthur Band.

The band gave concerts throughout the summer season at Old Colwyn and Rhos-on-Sea bandstands. It drew large crowds of locals and visitors. This picture was taken at Old Colwyn in 1955.

Even the traffic stopped for the band to play at Old Colwyn promenade on a summer evening in 1955.

A small group from Colwyn Band played in a scene from the White Horse Inn with the Colwyn Bay Light Opera Co. at the Prince of Wales Theatre in 1968.

*Right:* Colwyn Agricultural Show was held for many years in Eirias Park. Farmers from many parts would bring sheep, cattle and pigs to show and compete. A pony gymkhana was given on the football field. Trade stands were in abundance. The beer tent often ran dry. This picture is of Patrick Slattery and his mother Enid, 21 August 1958.

*Below:* Pat Collins Fairground near Colwyn Bay's station was a favourite spot for all ages. Here we see the roundabout, the wheel and miniature railway.

*Opposite above:* The big top was erected between the arena and entrance to Eirias Park and was filled twice daily for its shows by crowds who travelled from a wide area to enjoy the circus.

*Opposite below:* No circus was complete without its lions – the lion trainer was well in control here.

*Left:* The Peter Pan railway was loved by children of all ages; also the big wheel. Rides were only 6d in the 1950s. The fairground was demolished in the 1980s as part of the new Colwyn expressway.

*Below:* Bertram Mills Circus came to Eirias Park regularly. It had its own circus train that was left at Colwyn Bay sidings. The circus parade marched from the station headed by the band to Eirias Park. This inflatable elephant could be seen from miles around when it was flown high up to advertise the circus. This picture is from 1955.

This trio of artistes holds its audience spellbound as it ascends the heights of the big top.

Bertram Mills' high wire tightrope cyclists skilfully entertain a full house.

One of the Bertram Mills' Arab stallions going through its paces.

The elephants from the circus were exercised daily and walked from Eirias Park down to the beach as far as the pier.

*Above:* The elephants enjoying a 'dip' in the sea by Colwyn Bay Pier.

*Below:* A visit to Colwyn Bay seaside would not be complete without Professor Bert Codman's Punch and Judy show. His dog 'Toby' is perched on the Punch and Judy booth watching out for the crocodile. (Picture taken by Colwyn Bay Pier 1955)

The *Duchess of York* sailed daily throughout the summer providing weather and tide were favourable. It would go as far as Rhos-on-Sea Pier which can be seen on the horizon to the left of the picture. This picture was taken in July 1953.

The Old Colwyn breakwaters were ideal for children to 'dive off' as the tide cane in, July 1955.

THE SANDS, OLD COLWYN.

Old Colwyn sands were always a good place for digging and making sandcastles. These youngsters in 1926 were well protected from the sun.

The beach kiosk has closed for the night so we must go home for our tea at the end of a happy day on the beach at Old Colwyn. July 1955.

The Crosville offices on Conwy Road, Colwyn Bay was the stopping point for coaches that brought holidaymakers from Manchester and the Midlands. This picture was taken in August 1954.

The coaches arriving at the Crosville pick-up point. This was the scene on Saturday mornings throughout the summer season till the decline in tourism in the 1960s. This picture was taken in August 1954.

# Other local titles published by Tempus

## Rhyl
DAVE THOMPSON

Rhyl was born in 1794 as the craze for 'sea bathing' and 'taking the air' in summer resorts began to spread: it sprang into life with splendid villas, a terraced promenade and a railway which brought an ever-increasing number of visitors to the region. This absorbing collection of more than 200 old postcards and photographs provides a glimpse of Rhyl during the last century, and explores the town's transformation into a flourishing seaside resort.

978 07524 3783 5

## Chester
MICHAEL DAY AND PAT O'BRIEN

This collection of nearly 200 photographs charts the development of the walled city of Chester. Its history is recounted from its beginnings as a trading port to its development as an improtant escape from other industrial cities. The pictures reveal a bygone age in all its diversity. Memories will be evoked by scenes of busy streets, industry long forgotten and the faces of residents and workers through Chester's long history.

0 7524 0681 7

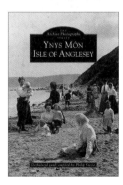

## Llandudno
DAVE THOMPSON

Llandudno has an intriguing history. Much of its past focuses on the magnificent Great Orme where St Tudno first established a church in the sixth century. This fascinating collection of over 200 photographs offers an in-depth look at the history of Llandudno over the last 150 years, taking the reader on a journey around the streets and buildings, recalling people and events which have shaped the character of the town.

978 7524 3683 8

## Yns Môn Isle of Anglesey
PHILIP STEELE

Most books of Anglesey's history show the island's ancient monuments, its castles and churches. This book of over 180 old photographs, reveals a more recent past when the romantic pictures produced by the engravers had been replaced by the more realistic images of the photographers. Their cameras captured the instant moment and those everyday events that historians rarely record.

978 07524 0310 9

If you are interested in purchasing other books published by Tempus, or in case you have difficulty finding any Tempus books in your local bookshop, you can also place orders directly through our website

**www.tempus-publishing.com**